I0880516

The School Rules

RULES IN THE CLASSROOM

By Paul Bloom

Gareth Stevens
CLASSROOM

Please visit our website, www.garethstevens.com. For a free color catalog of all our high-quality books, call toll free 1-800-542-2595 or fax 1-877-542-2596.

Library of Congress Cataloging-in-Publication Data

Bloom, Paul.
Rules in the classroom / by Paul Bloom.
p. cm. — (The school rules)
Includes index.
ISBN 978-1-4824-2641-0 (pbk.)
ISBN 978-1-4824-2642-7 (6 pack)
ISBN 978-1-4824-2643-4 (library binding)
1. Schools — Juvenile literature. 2. Etiquette for children and teenagers — Juvenile literature. 3. Classroom environment — Juvenile literature. I. Bloom, Paul, 1963-. II. Title.
LC210.B56 2016
372.18—d23

First Edition

Published in 2016 by
Gareth Stevens Publishing
111 East 14th Street, Suite 349
New York, NY 10003

Copyright © 2016 Gareth Stevens Publishing

Editor: Ryan Nagelhout
Designer: Laura Bowen

Photo credits: Cover, p. 1 kristian sekulic/E+/Getty Images; pp. 5, 24 (classroom) Fuse/Getty Images; p. 7 Jaren Jai Wicklund/Shutterstock.com; p. 9 michaeljung/Shutterstock.com; pp. 11, 13, 17, 24 (teacher) Pressmaster/Shutterstock.com; p. 15 Imcsike/Shutterstock.com; p. 19 Golden Pixels LLC/Shutterstock.com; p. 21 wavebreakmedia/Shutterstock.com; p. 23 Lisa Stirling/Digital Vision/Getty Images.

All rights reserved. No part of this book may be reproduced in any form without permission in writing from the publisher, except by a reviewer.

Printed in the United States of America

CPSIA compliance information: Batch #CS15GS: For further information contact Gareth Stevens, New York, New York at 1-800-542-2595.

Contents

Follow the
classroom rules.

Aa Bb Cc
Sight Words

Come to school
on time.

Work hard in class.

Listen to your teacher.

Follow any directions you are given.

Do not yell at others.

Raise your hand
if you want to talk.
This is how we
ask questions!

Listen when others talk!

Be nice to people
in class.

Help clean up!
It is nice to help
your teacher.

blue and yellow make green
Sticking

Words to Know

classroom

teacher

Index